JOURNEY OF WORDS

TWISHA RAY

This book has been published with all efforts taken to make the material error-free after the consent of the author. However, the author and the publisher do not assume and hereby disclaim any liability to any party for any loss, damage, or disruption caused by errors or omissions, whether such errors or omissions result from negligence, accident, or any other cause.

While every effort has been made to avoid any mistake or omission, this publication is being sold on the condition and understanding that neither the author nor the publishers or printers would be liable in any manner to any person by reason of any mistake or omission in this publication or for any action taken or omitted to be taken or advice rendered or accepted on the basis of this work. For any defect in printing or binding the publishers will be liable only to replace the defective copy by another copy of this work then available.

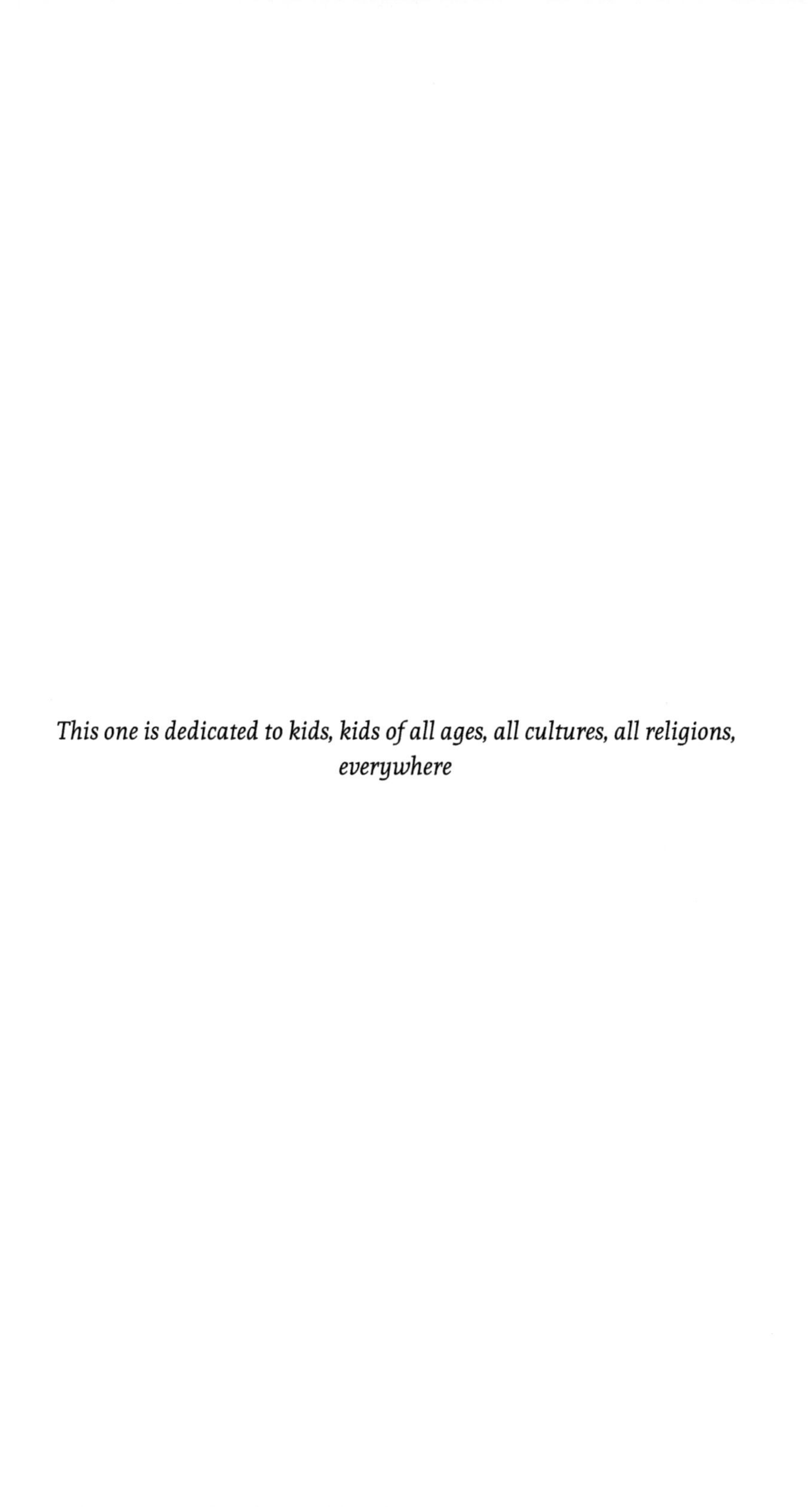

This one is dedicated to kids, kids of all ages, all cultures, all religions, everywhere

Contents

Foreword

By metaphor, I refer to one form of communication (along with stories, tales, and anecdotes) in the story genre in which an expression is taken from one field of experience and used to say something about another field of experience. To describe a bully as being as angry as a bear with a sore paw does not mean the bully and bear are literally alike but that the description, phrase, or story about the bear and its demeanor communicates an imaginative image of the bully and his or her behavior. It is this symbolic association that gives metaphors their literary and therapeutic potency. Metaphors in therapy and teaching are designed as a form of indirect, imaginative, and implied communication with clients, about experiences, processes, or outcomes that may help solve the child's literal problem and offer new means of coping. The therapist may talk about what a person needs to do to protect himself from a bear with a sore paw as a means for managing the circumstantial or emotional issues the listening child is encountering with a bully. Such metaphors may include stories, tales, anecdotes, jokes, proverbs, analogies, or other communications.

Preface

It is not my objective in this book to be too pedantic about the differential characteristics of stories, tales, and anecdotes. In fact, most times I will use the terms synonymously. Where I employ the words metaphor, healing story, or therapeutic tale, it is with the purpose of emphasizing that this is neither or just a casual, anecdotal account nor an inconsequential tale such as we may relate at a party. By metaphor or healing story I refer to a deliberately crafted story that has a clear, rational, and ethical therapeutic goal. It is, in other words, a tale that is based on our long human history of storytelling, grounded in the science of effective communication, demonstrating specific therapeutic relevance to the needs of the client, and told with the art of a good storyteller.

Once quotes, poetries, stories are written, in black and white, they tend to take on an immutable quality as though that is the way they always have been and always should be told. The reality is that stories are dynamic. They evolve, they change, and they adapt from teller to teller as well as from listener to listener Hopefully, you will discover that you never tell a similar story idea the same way twice, for the power of the story is often in its flexibility and adaptability to the needs of the listener and the listener's circumstances. Introduction xix Therefore, I cannot guarantee the quotes, poetries, stories in this book are as I originally heard them or initially developed them. Nor can I guarantee that the way you read them is the way I told them to my last client or will tell them to the next. May I suggest you see in the stories I have written their themes, ideas or meaning rather than the exact words with which they have been expressed in this format. These words were not designed to be told and retold as an actor may faithfully memorize and reiterate the words of a playwright. I hope you will allow the tales to evolve and, along with them, your own quotes, poetries, stories, and storytelling skills. Stories emerge from within us, they communicate about our own experiences, and, in turn, help define us as individuals. In stories it is possible for us, and our young clients, to find happiness and well-being, as well as the means for creating and maintaining positive emotional states.

Acknowledgements

Maa. BaBa, cr dadu, ila dida, Urmi ,ashtami and her family,somnath kaku and his family. all the people who makes me feel to write and to everyone who wishes/faces problem but can't express it to anyone.

PROLOGUE

Journey Of Words is an eclectic collection of modern quotes, poetries, stories on diverse themes like Life, Friendship, Love, Mindfulness, Nature, and Inspiration. The poems are an expression of my inner journey through life and its magical moments. The poems have a theme of mindfulness and meditativeness running through the compositions. The book wishes to inspire readers to take a stop in their busy lives and reflect on smaller things around us, which seem insignificant and yet, are so meaningful. To live every moment with higher consciousness and awareness. The poems speak of love & nostalgia on one hand and deriving inspiration from life on the other hand. The longer poems tell stories from imaginary days past. The poems on nature are reflections on the wonder of this beautiful world is your idcal companion to reflect and ruminate on, on a beautiful morning with your chai, or during the monsoon as you watch the rain fall, or on moonlit nights when you watch the full moon and fall in love once again. The poems are nothing special, just outpourings of our own heart put into words by me

I

God, are you listening

Oh God this burden broke my back,
I find out no specific than you to fallback.
Am worn-out of strolling to stay on here,
You do hear me as you are very nearby.
My devotion to you I renew again,
Thankful I am no be counted all the pain.
Your generosity to me is unimaginable,
Otherwise, my have faith would be unstable.
Went through hell and lower back many times,
Drowned in seas of sorrows sometimes.
Many storms have tried to root me out,
Useless when I had grown to be I used to be decreased out.
Since I am no longer for any use to this world,
Open my coronary coronary heart and show off me the exclusive world.
Cracked it is a bit thanks to these I loved,
Especially the one who used to be my beloved.
Oh God in broken hearts your presence,
Nullifies the total lot else's existence.
I do be given as real with that one day you will show,
Your moderate and then this darkish soul will glow.
Forget no longer the strength of the pen is stated to be,

Mightier than the sword in opposition to grave enemy.
Yet, whether or not you be militiaman or writer true,
From seeds of ink, watered by means of blood that freedom grew
You see as effective as pen and parchment be,
We nonetheless want the soldier to assist hold us free,
Some battles be fought on parchment with the pen,
But others require the blood and bravery of men.

II

HOGWARDS Is it real or dream ?

There is a magic region the place you can learn,
where instructors can be truthful however frequently stern.
Closed to Muggles and to non-magic Squibs,
most humans are signed from their toddler crib.
If I ought to get a bypass for Hogwarts school,
where I should have some exciting and play the fool.
I'd ask the sorting hat for Gryffindor,
where magic abilities are usually set to soar.
Talk to Hagrid about these Potter days,
and how life's modified now in so many ways.
Seek out these creatures' humans by no means see,
Some saved for training in herbology.
Heed voices from the artwork on the stair,
play Weasley hints we bought truthful and square.
Go purchasing in Hogsmeade for butter beer,
and if we're fortunate see the village seer.
At breakfast begin each day with comfortable cheer.
listen to magic discuss that I can hear,
Owls supply mail as they descend.

Watch friendships develop and spot the magic trends,
I would leap up to the sky on my new broom,
with Hippogriffs and dragons, I would zoom.
avoid the blunger - chase rather the snitch,
I would commence at closing to be a witch.
I'd exercise waving spherical my magic wand,
learn all about that world so a way beyond.
Cast spells and devour all flavoured jellybeans,
where every person simply has that magic gene.
If I ought to have a desire this would be mine,
just get me to that vicinity it truly is half of plus nine.

III

Butterfly @ race

If there used to be however a butterfly race
Not on the floor however in Outerspace,
On all the critters there is a number
To inform all drivers from every other.
    The climate is satisfactory no longer a raindrop
To motive the tournament to have to stop,
So all the butterflies they line up
To take a look at their skills and their luck.
    That very arm that holds the flag
It starts offevolved the race however with a wag,
Eyes for sight and wings for flight
The nascar race has come to light.
    Its wing to wing as drivers set sail
On the invisible tune it is tail to tail,
Round and spherical all the critters go
Who will be the one to steal the show.
    The winner is the first butterfly home
That first butterfly to move the gate,
Don't want to talk his well-known name
For anyone is aware of that eighty-eight.

IV

Sparkling Wave

An thing of risk now not for the meek.
Living for the second I as soon as did seek...
    I surfed the waves when I was once young,
White-crested demons I rode among.
Still hear their indignant roar to this very day,
Feel their energy and sharp sea-salt spray.
    Sometimes you wipe-out, every now and then you win.
Those euphoric instances driving one all the way in.
But the mystical Ninth Wave is the one I crave,
It'll feel hesitation and drag you to the grave.
    Wave upon wave every mightier than the last,
Till remaining a ninth one its energy unsurpassed.
So sharpen your wits if you dare journey upon one,
And bang your drum loudly for your life's begun.

V

Sa, Re, Ga, Ma, Pa, Dha,Ni/ Do,Re,Mi,Fa,So,La Fi,Ti- Are you hearing it my soul ?

Everything in track is a series of sound frequencies,
Every word has its personal special vibration and colour.
Some humans are blessed with ideal pitch,
And they can right away inform if some thing is out of key.

Everything in this world emit their very own special frequency,
Is life's reason all about discovering the relative pitch?
Are we supposed to locate anyone special,
Who will admire the identical songs as us?

Does the universe assist us tune in our destiny,
And show us delicate signs and symptoms on what our future is.
Are some human beings simply naturally top at something,
Or did they recognize that is their calling in life?

Looking returned in my life, I have completed various things.
But how come my soul is nevertheless tone deaf?
My music is almost end and I surprise if,
I will ever discover my relative pitch in life?

How about you? Have you discovered out
What frequency your soul sings?

VI

Oh Mountains

Climbing a mountain used to be such a gorgeous feeling,
The view used to be so majestic but additionally scary.
It was once such a humbling experience,
Because it reminded me of what existence is.
Climbing to the pinnacle represents life,
The direction used to be now not linear and easy.
I had to center of attention on each step and breath,
Because It was once brutal, difficult and harsh.
In lifestyles some human beings will without difficulty attain the peak
And others will stumble and lose their strength.
Unfortunately, I did now not reached the absolute best point
But my buddies who cheered me on melted my heart.
Because it reminded me of the authentic motive in life.
I used to be too centered on accomplishing my ambitions,
And I misplaced sight of the necessary phase of life.
Someday when I attain the summit,
A steep slope down to the bed
A nonetheless lake shaped from watersheds
Filled with raindrops crystal clear
Reflected splendor that appears

The air so sparkling it fills my lungs
Its heady scent sensed with my tongue
Flowers pollinate from the bees
And fragrance lingers in the breeze
This hidden treasure, my escape
To cover from all of life's pink tape
I experience so sorry for man one day
Because quickly he'll take this all away
I will cherish the stunning scenery,
with my love ones.

VII

Accepting truth

'I completely admire my mother for raising a child with cerebral palsy at home'

– Natalia Vodianova

s I was once on foot toward the departmental store, abruptly I heard my title being known as out. On turning again I noticed a lady, however for a minute ought to now not understand her. Very quickly it struck me that she was once a true buddy of mine in my college days. Yes, Chaaya reappeared in my lifestyles after a lengthy hole of 25 years. Since each of us had been strolling round with our morning chores that day, after replacing some pleasantries, we constant up a date for a lengthy chat the following week.

With reminiscences of our carefree faculty days the place we gossiped, shared secrets, poured out our problems, giggled over stupid jokes, right here we have been searching ahead to assembly with every different in a restaurant in Mumbai. Circumstances modified and in the pre-social-networking generation we steadily drifted aside and ultimately misplaced contact with one another. The day of our assembly sooner or later dawned and all excited seeing that morning I went out to meet my pal in the evening. There she was once with a beaming smile and we rushed into every other's arms. In an instant, time acquired reversed, and it used to be with a outstanding feeling of being excessive on recollections that we dug into our reminiscence pool and exchanged 'what we did' stories.

It used to be whilst we have been catching up on the years between then and now, updating every different on our lives and households that Chaaya noted about her 15-year-old daughter, Dolly, who had cerebral palsy (CP), following problems at birth.

"Is this hopeless?" Chaaya requested upon mastering about Dolly's diagnosis. Chaaya knew there was once a opportunity that Dolly may want to have problems—she was once born prematurely—but she in no way imagined the difficulties that lay ahead. Though Dolly appeared first-rate at first, various months later Chaaya commenced to word that every so often Dolly appeared very floppy, nearly like a rag doll. Other times, she appeared to stiffen. "I knew she wasn't hitting the equal increase and motor milestones like my older daughter," stated Chaaya.

Several doctors' appointments later on, she in the end acquired a prognosis of cerebral palsy. "I bear in mind these first days, weeks, months and years after receiving the analysis and how I felt. So you can think about how the ultimate years have been — I am on 24/7 support," stated Chaaya with a mild smile. "I haven't had an awful lot time for socializing. This is the first time in a lengthy length that I have set apart some time to capture up with buddies and relatives. My husband, in-laws, mom and sister are taking care of my daughter, whilst I am taking this clean break. The trip of CP is a lesson in purposive love, whilst all alongside accepting and managing your child's current conditions," concluded she.

Soon after Chaaya left, I saved mulling over this hassle and it compelled me to do some lookup on this problem of cerebral palsy, a neurological sickness that seems in infancy or early childhood owing to harm to the growing brain, however does now not irritate over time. It completely influences physique motion and muscle coordination, and is accompanied by way of some diploma of intellectual retardation. Current lookup suggests the majority of CP instances end result from both atypical talent improvement or

Genius damage prior to beginning or all through labour and delivery. Accidents, abuse, clinical malpractice, negligence, infections, and damage are some recognised threat elements that may additionally lead to CP.

In extreme cases, signs and symptoms are normally immediate. In slight cases, however, it can also take months or even years earlier than you will be capable to word symptoms. However, the signs and symptoms are exceptional from the signs, and a health practitioner commonly diagnoses the disease based totally upon each signs and symptoms and symptoms. A signal of cerebral palsy can be detecting malformations in the brain, whilst a symptom can be how a baby feels, moves, and acts. Regardless, if the signs and symptoms are now not obvious immediately, they nearly usually floor by means of 3-5 years of age. Majority of youth with CP are born with it.

The child's analysis of cerebral palsy is a lifelong experience of recurrent adversity eliciting a collection of individualized responses. These responses consist of the timing of the diagnosis; and the preliminary response of anger; denial; guilt; blame; and frustration. The truth of the analysis elicits pain, sorrow and loss of desires whereas adaptation encompasses acceptance and empowerment. Mothers show a spirit of advocacy for their baby and reveal non-public increase thru the experience. Awareness of society's ambivalence, provides to the stress the households sense inside themselves.

The guardian of a infant with cerebral palsy is commonly the first to be aware these symptoms and to realise that the toddler is now not creating normally. The signs and symptoms of cerebral palsy differ broadly and can vary from moderate to severe. Some human beings with the situation are intellectually impaired, however many have no intellectual deficits at all. Cerebral palsy reasons reflex moves that a man or woman is unable to manipulate and, muscle tightness that can also have an effect on components or all of the body. Intellectual disability, seizures, and imaginative and prescient and listening to troubles can occur.

When we pause to think about the reality that this is only one of the many debilitating problems of this type that can have an effect on kiddies and teenagers and proceed into adulthood, it drives domestic the reality that there are many moms and caregivers who play this 24/7 aid role, with restrained or no time for themselves or their careers or interests. The mothering journey necessitates dealing with many kinds of burden including: usually some thing to hurdle, bodily worrying routine, complicated competencies, persistent worry, insufficient respite time and monetary issues. Support from others is preferred however it is now not constantly received. Typical household existence is disrupted ensuing in altered relationships amongst household individuals which include different children, husband and parents. But the truth stays that moms shoulder the bulk of the responsibility, with no expectations or boundaries, pushed by using pure, selfless love. Globally, over 17 million humans have cerebral palsy and so it follows that we have over 17 million moms and caregivers on carrier spherical the clock.

It is vital to apprehend cerebral palsy signs and symptoms as quickly as possible, as the beforehand the disease is diagnosed, the higher probabilities you will have in lowering the severity of disabilities related with the disorder. There is no therapy for cerebral palsy, however early intervention can measurably enhance your child's capability to manipulate the condition. Cerebral Palsy is now not a ailment – it is really a time period used to describe a vary of stipulations that commonly reason bodily impairment. Some redress that are possible, relying on the severity of the problem, are bodily and occupational therapy; speech therapy; tablets to manage seizures, loosen up muscle spasms and alleviate pain; surgical procedure to right abnormalities or launch tight muscles; braces and different orthotic devices, wheelchairs and rolling walkers, and verbal exchange aids. Treatment, therapy, surgery, medicines and assistive science can assist maximize independence, decrease barriers, expand inclusion and as a consequence lead to an improved satisfactory of life. So far, the remedy alternative for CP is to manipulate the signs of the ailment. However, in current times, scientists and researchers global have began to discover stem mobile remedy as a workable remedy alternative for CP patients.

The spirit of womanhood wants to be saluted as it shines in all its glory right here and wishes cognizance with reverence. I am reminded of this extremely good quote: "The sun, moon, and stars in the sky may also shine for trillions of years like the gentle flickering small candlelight, that doesn't get put out in seasons of wind and storm. True splendor and perfectionism in love are like belief that can by no means be banished, hope that can in no way die." Right now three matters remain: faith, hope, and love. But the biggest of these is love.

There is no denying the reality that the starting of this ride is hard, however with dedication to your child, and determination, you will cross ahead and discover that you have internal sources you in no way knew existed. As I am in steady contact with my pal now, I am conscious of the problem in which she is placed. She used to be a carefree individual these days, however now she has gone through a radical change. I am humbled and proud due to the fact of her. Proud due to the fact of the character she is nowadays and humbled via the fantastic qualities, which consist of courage; patience; perseverance and stoic acceptance; advantageous attitude; tolerance closer to an inhuman society; the ever inclined nature to assist and information others in a comparable regular care-giving situation; and the efforts closer to growing people's focus of this problem, which she has developed all through this onerous journey

You can be your child's first-class recommend in the months and years to come, making sure that he or she receives the care that is needed. The greater you know, the higher organized you will be to assist your child. This is mainly vital in the case of cerebral palsy, which is a complicated circumstance with a huge vary of feasible signs and symptoms and complications. The appropriate information is that there are now many choices for youth with cerebral palsy and their mother and father and caregivers, in phrases of scientific and surgical treatments, realistic assist and social care support, and additionally accessible is a mine of ingenious information.

VIII

Hapless Rose

It was once a wet dusk. The total Eden district of Pernith city used to be dwindled below the gloom of rain. The black sheath of David resembled the shadow of the sky, as he strolled on the street. David was once an adolescent, living by myself in a one-room apartment, which he should barely afford. He was once working in a personal company which granted him a much less salary. That very evening, David used to be swiftly strolling as it used to be raining extremely. It was once eight at night.

David stepped into a keep at the nook the street. It was once Legal Store and was once about to get closed simply when David entered. "Can I have a cigarette please?", requested David, searching graspingly at Steve, the shopkeeper.

"Sure, however its my closing time now. Come the subsequent day", answered Steve in an oblivious manner.

"But I choose solely one, its already raining seeing that morning and most of the shops are closed nearby.....I can beg you for this if you favor me to...". David used to be needy for that cigarette. Steve, was once in a hurry to shut his save as it was once raining endlessly.

Unwillingly, Steve provided a cigarette to David, "Here you go".

David took the cigarette in his hand and seemed for a lighter in his pockets. He should now not get that. Now. Steve was once stepping out of the save simply then David uttered, “Do you maintain a lighter with you”.

Steve used to be aggravated at this and answered, “You requested me for a cigarette and you don’t hold a lighter with you.... strange!”. Steve supplied David with the lighter. Just when the lighter blew up, the rain went greater sense.

“It appears the rain is long-lasting. We shall wait right here for some time. What do you assume Mr...... What’s your title by using the way?”

Steve seemed at David in a displeased way. “I’m Steve”, answered Steve sitting on a bench inner the store. It was once David who made Steve to wait unwillingly, uselessly. David additionally entered except any allowance. Both of them had been seated on the identical bench. The entire city used to be being showered by means of torrent of rain. The cigarette used to be fuming the atmosphere.

“Can I locate a area to grasp up my sheath....it’s wet”, David asked. Steve pointed at a hanger which was once at the bottom of the door.

It was once midnight. David commenced to slumber, mendacity on the bench. Sitting beside, Steve was once aggravated as he used to be confused with this premature night, and that too due to the fact of the one beside him.

The night time exceeded anyhow. It rained the complete night. Steve was once conscious for the night time whilst David had a precise slumber.

“Get up younger man, you had a desirable time here”, Steve poked David with a stick. David bought up in a slow manner and appeared out. “Oh God, what’s the time....”, “7, Mr David”, Steve said. David stood up rapidly and took up his sheath. It was once Monday and he had to go to his place of business earlier. So, he fixed-up himself and used to be stepping out of the store. Steve opened the door and let him leave. As he used to be leaving, a harsh voice stopped him,”You have to pay me David”, David grew to become round and it was once Steve. David gave a smile and said, “pay for what?”.

“For that one cigarette. It used to be really worth 5 Penny.”

“What! 5....but it expenses solely 3”, David said.

“Time is extra valuable sir. You took my complete night time uselessly.”

“And that one night time expenses two penny.... isn’t it weird”.

David used to be already in a hurry however Steve was once cussed at his point. He stored on arguing for some time and agreed to take three penny for the cigarette only. David additionally agreed to pay him the money. He seemed into his pockets however used to be now not capable to get whatever out of it. David used to be out of pocket that time. He instructed this to Steve.

“Then why did you ask for a want when you’re now not having something to pay for it....what if I do this to you!”

David seemed Steve for amnesty however Steve stored on humiliating David.

At last, David concluded, “Okay listen, proper now I have to go to my workplace. While returning in the evening, I shall supply you your cash for sure. Calm down!”

Steve appeared at David with anger. David managed to go away in any case and reached at his apartment. It was once eight now. His room was once depressing and he attired himself in a nicely manner and moved out. He wasn’t having some thing to take in his breakfast. Not even a single penny!

David reached his office. There he was once given a reward for his exact work. The reward used to be a rose given by means of his manager. “David, I provide you this rose as your subsequent month salary. Its a magical rose blessed with positive powers that would make you richer day by way of day. You ought to be satisfied to take it. Wherever you go, this rose will supply you wealth.”, the supervisor stated to David.

In the dusk, David with blushes on his face, moved out from office, taking the reward with pride. David used to be delighted. He was once wondering about the subsequent month which would be spent with superb comfort. As he was once strolling on the road in the front of his apartment, he was once interrupted by way of a voice,"hey you, younger man David", it used to be Steve.

David grew to become round and Steve's furios face made him keep in mind the final night. No quicker has David commenced with his words, Steve uttered, "I favor my money. You promised me to supply in the evening. May I have it...".

David was once speechless. He should no longer suppose what to do. All he was once having used to be that treasured rose. Steve stored on criticising David in the front of everybody round there. David, unwillingly, took out the rose and said, "All I have with me is this. If you are going to receive it, you can. Its no longer an regular one. It's a magical rose....".

David defined to the shopkeeper the whole lot about the rose. After listening all these, Steve laughed at David pointing toward the rose, " How can a rose make human beings rich?"

Steve widespread the rose as he was once no longer having any different alternatives. David said,"Its now not simply a rose, genuinely its my life's one month. Its one month happiness to that I am giving you."

David, with a heavy heart, moved towarst his condo and Steve went into his keep with the rose. He concept for a while,"How can a rose make me rich? Its all my fault. I ought to no longer have been so mild with him yesterday. He made me fool. "

Thinking this, he flinged the rose on the road in the front of the store. As the rose touched the harsh street surface, it began to rain closely as yesterday.

IX

It's Just a begining

Four days earlier than marriage:-

They are assembly for the first time. They have now not viewed every different even in the picture. Reason? He is her family's desire and she wishes to be given him blindly. On the different hand, he is now not joyful with this marriage. So he has no activity in seeing her. He has come to inform her the truth.

"Listen, I have no activity in this marriage," He said. "I used to be in a serious relationship before. She left me or we broke up that does now not suggest that I will substitute her. I nevertheless love her and I can't supply that location to anybody else. For my family, I can't flip down this proposal. I prefer you to reject me and simply say no to this marriage and I have now not instructed you that you are now not beautiful. We don't have any future together. You don't recognize what love is. He left. "

Four days after marriage:-

It used to be so referred to as first night time for each and every couple to emerge as of every other. She was once in her dream bridal lehenga. Her forearm crammed with golden bangles. Palm-filled with mehndi graph hiding his identify in it. He has to discover it out today. She waits, waits and waits. Till morning he did no longer come. He used to be taking part in alcohol with buddies for the complete night.

Fourteen days after marriage:-

He barely appears at her. He doesn't choose to. Let her do what she is doing. He is in no temper in relieving his ego. Even he warned her the final result however she used to be displaying her silent happiness. Yeah, its actual he used to be now not having any eye contact with her however used to be now not in a position to withstand ownself from staring at her from in the back of when she was once busy in serving relatives, caring for his parents. She used to be searching glad for what she had obtained from this marriage.

Forty days after marriage:-

He was once no longer roaming late night time with friends. In spite of his ego, some thing used to be changing there. Those days, he used to be staying busy looking at at her when she used to be in the kitchen, whilst she relaxed, the time she washes and folds his garments when she busy gossiping with her sister in-law. He did now not favor to say her thank you and sorry however in any case he stated that. Maybe he saved her head on his chest on that day when she was once struggling from fever, hugged her and whispered in her ear. He discovered her so soft, so lovable and she had a infantile seem when she used to be in his arms.

Fourteen months after marriage:-

Finding a actual love is no longer that easy. As they say, "It's higher to be with anybody who loves you as an alternative to whom you love". He determined it inner his home, beneath the roof above the bed. Nowadays they are speaking a lot. She in no way insists him to remain at domestic nor to come early in night however he has no cause to continue to be out. He needs her to take outdoor and dine her dinner at the nice restaurant in the metropolis and make her buying from the quality purchasing complex. The endless affection makes his coronary heart alive that used to be in the coma from long. It recovered and thanked her each and every time it beats. "I usually prefer to be with you" he promised her million times.

Forty months after marriage:-

He is equipped to receive the venture that each person receives as soon as in a existence with the aid of turning into a father. In between these few months, he has verified himself as a accurate husband. As she is pregnant now, he is cooking for her, medicating her on time, storing a range of fruits and greens on the refrigerator, reducing her nails, sharpening them with specific nail colors, making her hear to a story and lot stuff for his love. Maybe it will remind you all of your one.

Fourteen 12 months after marriage:-

They are the dad or mum of two. With a lovely daughter and a blessed son, their household is complete. They have each happiness. She is nonetheless the most lovely girl for him and he thanks her for constantly being there with him.

Forty yr after marriage:-

Somewhere in an historic age home, she is mendacity on the mattress and he is sitting there letting his hand in her hand. He barely searching around. He left the whole thing in the back of and his soul mate is dying. Doctors said, “this is age impact and she has now not plenty time”. She is so susceptible that she even can’t open her eyes. Keeping her head on his lap, he is wiping her tears and reminding what he promised to her.

How they reached right here is a frequent story for everyone. But as they stated each went hand in hand. As promised.

X

Daksh's adventure

Daksh is a lovable chubby boy, who attracts everyone's interest at first sight due to his bubbly nature and the dependancy of imparting his personal organized sweets to all people he meets. Actually when he was once a great deal younger, he tried to prepare dinner strawberry yoghurt flavored bubble gum which exploded as some thing may have long past incorrect whilst cooking. But from then onwards he regularly increased his competencies through persevering with training his ardour of cooking.

Actually the best wish of Daksh is to be the great sweet producer of the u . s . a . in future. As a small child he no longer solely loves to consume candies, however additionally loves to prepare dinner them himself. His knack in cooking is inherited from his father, who works as the Chief Chef of the royal kitchen in the palace of the king of his land. But lamentably his father does now not guide his goal to be a top candy-maker as in accordance to him candy-making can't be counted as actual cooking at all; although secretly he is proud for his son's ardour to work in kitchen. Daksh loves cooking sweet so an awful lot that even his bike consists of a giant case simply in the back of the handles, which consists of each fundamental object for cooking so that he can cook dinner a sweet every time he feels like.

He is significantly cherished and admired through his buddies who continually reward his cooked sweets and prefer his organisation for his humorous nature. They preserve on inspiring him on his ambition to be the biggest candy-maker of the land. Daksh secretly needs to make a wonderland one day, which will be full of specific sorts of tasty candies, all cooked with the aid of him. He spends his amusement time by means of studying cookery books or staring at cookery indicates coming up on television. Hence his candy-making competencies have upgraded pretty a lot due to the fact his first trial in childhood. Since he stays in the royal palace with his mother and father due to his father's job, he constantly has the get admission to to the royal kitchen the place typically he receives the entirety that he wants to cook dinner a sweet or a desert.

One day he organized a special kind of candy, based totally on a recipe he determined in a book. It used to be a lemon flavored sweet with a milk chocolate coating. He saved the plate of freshly organized chocolates close to the window, ready the sweets to cool down earlier than he should style them. He was once sitting in his find out about desk and doing his homework for the subsequent day, when all at once he heard a sound coming from the window. He grew to become spherical rapidly and noticed a particularly little chicken pecking at his chocolates with its tiny purple beak. Daksh allowed the chicken to proceed consuming the candies, as he usually preferred all of us who would recognize his cooking. Suddenly the little blue chook grew to become into a fairy carrying blue robe and having blue wings too!! Billy used to be speechless through this surprise, when the fairy spoke to him very sweetly. She informed him that she was once very thrilled with him due to the fact he allowed her to consume his goodies which he cooked with so an awful lot effort. The blue fairy supplied to take him to the Fairyland as his reward of kindness.

Daksh was once very joyful and of direction he agreed. The blue fairy held his hand and flew off! Within a few minutes, they reached a awesome land, which Daksh realized used to be the Fairyland. There he met with many different stunning fairies. They determined to exhibit him the entire Fairyland took him up on a flying boat. He was once amazed by using the wonderful splendor of this land with giant colourful vegetation in the gardens, waterfalls and inexperienced meadows with golden and silvery coloured trees. Then he used to be taken to a vicinity the place he noticed mounds of goodies of quite a number kinds, many of which he had in no way even heard of. He used to be advised that he ought to devour and additionally take with him as a whole lot sweet he wanted. But Daksh desired to understand the recipes of these special candies, so that he should put together them himself after going returned home. He in a well mannered way requested the Fairy Queen if he may want to have these recipes. She used to be thrilled with his honesty and touched him with her magic-wand. Instantly he observed that all these recipes had been in his intelligence and he should keep in mind them anytime! Then the blue fairy took him returned to his bedroom.

When he obtained up early subsequent morning, he first notion that he simply had a fantastic dream about the fairies. But when he noticed these ordinary looking goodies on his bed-side table, he realized that simply he had travelled to the Fairyland the preceding night! He without delay went to the kitchen after breakfast and tried to take into account the recipes of these gorgeous sweets and cookies he noticed in Fairyland. To his amazement, Daksh discovered that he should be mindful precisely all these recipes very easily.

With his father's permission, he shortly cooked up a tasty pie and a scrumptious candy. Both the sweets smelled so good, that Daksh requested his father if these new objects ought to be served as deserts to the king and queen. After an awful lot hesitation his father in the end agreed. Hence after the most important route of the lunch, Daksh's father served his son's cooked dishes to the royal couple. The king and queen each have been notably thrilled to style these new items. They praised Daksh's father for cooking some thing so delicious, which they had in no way tasted before! Then their Chief Chef published the fact that these deserts had been virtually cooked by using his eleven yr historic son Daksh

Both king and queen have been speechless to hear this wonderful news!! They referred to as Billy and praised his superb cooking intelligence wholeheartedly. Billy knowledgeable them about his ambition to be the biggest sweet maker of the land. The king guaranteed him of all viable assist in his way toward the fulfilment of his purpose of life. The queen advised that they have been proud to have such a brilliantly gifted boy in their kingdom! Even his father admitted that Billy had really received knack for making candy dishes, which should make him the great candy-man of their planet! Thereby all and sundry is aware of Billy as the most gifted candy-manufacturing boy in the country. Daksh usually thanks the fairies from his coronary heart for their gigantic assist in pleasant his best desire.

XI
Little Goblin

Baba Yaga used to be a fairy. Or as a substitute she ought to say she used to be. Time used to be passing inexorably, and one day she realized that no one wishes her and in truth she was once unemployed. In the merciless capitalistic world personnel desired youthful and extra alluring women. Old fairy clearly didn't healthy the market needs. In fact, her buddies had a job even being a good deal older from her, however she observed her herbal way of existence extra noble-minded than the use of Botox injections simply to seem to be youthful and have a job.

Some fellow fairies genuinely exaggerated with most modern cosmetology techniques. Of course, every one of them should use a easy magic phantasm to seem younger, however it would work solely for anyone except any magic abilities. Everyone who had any thought about magic would effortlessly discover that the given fairy used to be the use of phantasm spells, and if different fellow fairies did it they would by no means let such a fairy go. She would turn out to be a ideal challenge for gossips for many weeks. Thus plastic surgical operation appeared to be the solely way for an historical fairy to hold her role on the market. Nevertheless, Baba Yaga didn't favor to hear about such solution.

She had her pride. Indeed, she got here from a noble household of fairies. Her grandmother was once the Fairy Godmother who had helped Cinderella herself! Her different ancestors additionally performed imperative roles in many much less regarded tales. Even even though the Wicked Queen who oppressed Snow White used to be additionally cognate with Baba Yaga, that used to be the solely witch in the entire family.

Sad, with her head down, Baba Yaga was once strolling down the street, dressed in a thick brown coat, which blanketed additionally her subtle wings. Her wand and magic books had been interior her valise. The bloodless autumn climate aggravated her depression. She had no region to go. In the magic forest, the domestic of all fairies, she felt a lot unwanted, a stranger amidst her fairy mates, solely apparently pleasant to her. Moreover, the fairy memories characters had been now not entitled to a pension.

Filled with melancholic mood, she used to be passing the gravcyard. "If no one needs me, then possibly I'll relaxation right here underneath the ground. No one will word anyway." She crossed the gate.

Several meters in addition she noticed a younger priest standing close to the grave. He didn't appear completely happy either. Once he noticed her, he said:

"Oh, dear! Can you think about such a savagery and vandalism? I wager that in your days it would be impossible."

Thanks for noticing my age, idea she. No marvel you don't have a wife. Which one would stand such a 'gentleman'?

She seemed at the tombs. Indeed, any person profaned them.

"There should have been a satanic feast closing night." defined the priest. "Look at these useless cats, and crosses upside down. Horror!"

Baba Yaga abruptly revived. The scene virtually impressed her.

"I would train a lesson to such imbeciles!" shouted she. "Dumb stripling's!"

"Would you?" requested the priest. "Very well! I appoint you. You will shield the graveyard."

Baba Yaga was once startled at his words, however a minute later she observed it a appropriate idea. After all, she had to earn cash somehow.

"I am Father Matthew. The parish can additionally furnish lodging for you. The room adjoining to the chapel is tremendously high-quality and warm, albeit no longer too big. And of path you will have a commercial enterprise mobile. Call the police in case of any night time visitors."

The priest confirmed her her room and they signed an agreement.

The first week nothing befell at night. The 2nd week on Tuesday used to be a brilliant storm over the graveyard. The sky used to be thundering terribly. Contours of leafless bushes (it used to be autumn) illuminated by using lightnings regarded genuinely spooky. Yet, the fairy wasn't afraid at all. She felt cozy and heat in her small room.

However, the next night time she couldn't sleep at all, even regardless of analyzing all the boring books she had. The air after the rain ought to nonetheless be fresh, she thought, and determined to go for a brief walk. She took her coat and left. Occasionally she observed her magic wand in the internal pocket. Normally it ought to have been in the valise, however she determined now not to take off the coat, which she simply took on, and quickly left to breathe the clean air.

The kick back of the night time was, indeed, in some way pleasant, and it was once fine to breathe the humid air shopping amongst the graves.

Suddenly she noticed a small hearth in a far-off phase of the necropolis, and headed closer to it. Having nearly approached the supply of the fire, she observed numerous candles burning in the corners of a pink two-meter-diameter pentagram. Three younger guys have been standing round the satanic symbol, one of them maintaining a cat. Once she got here every other few steps closer, she seen the cat held by means of the man was once bleeding.

The devil's worshipper is the use of cat's blood to make a purple circle round the pentagram! concept she.

Two different guys held a cage with some other cat, ready to be sacrificed in the horrible ritual too.

The bitter scent of animal's blood used to be blended with refined scent of melted candle wax and the sparkling air. Baba Yaga felt anger burning in her heart.

"What are you doing, dull kids!" shouted she.

Not ready for an answer, she took her magic wand from the internal pocket of her coat. Without a phrase she despatched three magic sparks in the direction of the Satanists. Hit with magical bullets, they shouted and began running. Fairy used to be following them for a minute, however due to her bad bodily situation in her ancient years she had no risk to trap them. Thus she despatched the different three sparks with her wand which burned Satanists' butts, and she lower back to the website online of the profanation.

It was once too late to assist the terrible little cat, sacrificed through the devil's servants; the animal was once dead. She launched some other cat from the cage. The small, red, furry creature was once searching at her with its large eyes precisely like in the scene from the "Shrek" movie. The cat regarded to apprehend that Baba Yaga had saved him from disgraceful death.

Soon Father Matthew got here to the web page of fairy's hostilities with Satanists. He had been alarmed with screams for the duration of their retreat. He regarded round and nodded his head.

"Great job, Baba Yaga! I knew I should rely on you!" stated he.

She smiled decently...

She named her cat Philemo, the identify she determined very special. Days had been passing and the fairy used to be truely relaxed with her new life. Not solely had she a devoted friend, the cat, which located Baba Yaga his saviour however she used to be additionally revered via the priest, her boss. Father Matthew cited her braveness for the duration of his severa sermons, and confirmed it as a right instance to imitate. Nevertheless, the height of her profession was once nonetheless to come...

One day she examine an article in a newspaper about a collection of mysterious deaths. Seven human beings had already been determined died in comparable circumstances. All seven had exceeded away from blood shortage, and the police collectively with the fitness provider have been inspecting if they have been murdered or died for some abnormal disease.

Baba Yaga, however, had her suspect as quickly as she had completed analyzing the article. She remembered meting him countless instances when he used to be returning to his grave in the morning. The tomb was once in the lane of distinctly historic sepulchres.

The man should have been a nobleman throughout his life, idea she. A be counted or some thing like that...

Of course, each and every time she met him, he used to be reprimanded for braking cemetery regulations.

"The first factor says that the graveyard is a location of everlasting relaxation for the dead. Thus, anyone who leaves his grave breaks this point." she advised him various times, however the rely simply nodded his head and didn't thinking to observe the rules. Bloated aristocrat!

One day she seen Philemo, her cat, behaved one way or the other weird, so she took it for a walk... and of direction met the matter returning with his lips all red.

"Yes, it ought to be him! He's accountable for this vampirism." notion she in the end. " Bloody Dracula!"

She instructed about her supposition to Father Matthew. His response was once quick; he made one cellphone name and the exorcist arrived to deal with the situation. The police arrived soon, too.

The entire operation was once quick. The priest and the exorcist opened the grave and the coffin, put an aspen stake in vampire's coronary heart and closed everything. The police officer made a report.

Indeed, the mysterious deaths ceased.

When three weeks surpassed except any victims, the police closed the case. The chief of the police branch described the case answer to the mayor and the mayor determined to reward the fairy. She grew to be the honourable citizen and acquired a medal. For taking section in revealing Dracula's responsible Philemo used to be rewarded with a tasty liver dish...

Now Baba Yaga used to be so famous that each person desired to go to her and make a photograph together. The media favored interviews. Crowds visited the cemetery, which the priest didn't like an awful lot as they have been traumatic the peace of the dead.

Nevertheless, no matter her recognition the fairy usually used to be capable to discover time to meet with everyday people.

One day a farmer Joseph visited her with an abnormal problem. His favourite canine Azor, the pal of the complete household and the defender of the farm, had died.

"I am afraid I can do nothing now. This negative animal is actually dead." stated Baba Yaga.

"But you comprehend the magic. I accept as true with you can revive Azor!"

"Sir! This requires necromancy skills. My speciality is completely different."

"Oh dear! He used to be such a precise animal. Always when a bunch of colleagues visited me, he used to be very happy, even even though my spouse simply was once not. Please, perhaps there is at least a small chance..."

"Well... when I had been at school, I had attended the necromancy classes, however simply for one semester. Nevertheless, my contract with Father Matthew doesn't permit me to use black magic in my work."

The farmer was once neglecting, anyway. He described his relation with the canine and his affection to the animal. Finally he noticed Philemo on the pinnacle of furnace, who simply woke up.

He determined to use the cat as his argument.

“How would you experience if your cat surpassed away? Wouldn’t you leave out it? Besides, you are the fairy and you are about to do appropriate deeds. Aren’t you?”

“Well... all right, however please thinking that I have a little trip in the necromancy, so the ritual can definitely no longer work.”

“Please, simply do your best...”

As so did she. The farmer helped the fairy to put together everything. They put the canine on the desk in Baba Yaga’s room and surrounded it’s physique with candles.

They began the ritual at night. It was once full moon.

“I have examine in my faculty guide that the most environment friendly approach of reviving a lifeless physique is medical doctor Frankenstein’s. However, we don’t have ample voltage in this room, so I have to attempt traditional spells.”

She fanned quite a few pages of her e book and located the perfect incantation.

„The e book is historic and I can’t examine some letters.” advised fairy to farmer Joseph. ”Maybe you should have a seem to be with your younger eyes.”

„Hmm... Abra-cadabra or Adra-acabra... I’m now not sure... I wager the 2nd one.”

Fairy approached the dog.

„Adra-acabra” stated she.

Flames of the candles steadily diminished and the wind used to be howling outside.

„Come on doggy. Stand up!” stated she.

It thoudered once, then twice, and the physique of the animal used to be shaking.

Something is wrong... thinking fairy.

„Adra-acabra” she repeated.

The canine was once trembling and his physique was once progressively transforming. It grew better and bigger. Suddenly it arose, however it didn’t seem to be like a canine anymore.

"Oh dead! Oh no! Oh no! Oh no!" shouted Baba Yaga." It used to be a incorrect spell! The animal has converted into a werewolf! I must have used the different spell!"

The werewolf howled. Baba Yaga was once terrified, and so was once the farmer.

The beast used to be coming nearer and nearer to them. Once the werewolf surpassed close to the window, it felt the mild of the full moon on its cheek. It appeared at the moon and left the room, simply like it heard some call.

Baba Yaga and the farmer have been standing quite a few extra minutes except any move, paralysed with the fear.

Soon father Matthew came.

"Did you see it? Some beast simply ran from the graveyard."

He seemed at the desk and seen the ritual. Quickly he put two and two together.

"Baba Yaga! So... it used to be you who known as the beast, right? And what about our contract?" shouted he on the terrible terrified ancient lady...

Fortunately the werewolf was once long gone from the city and inhabited the forest. When the authorities realized about it, the wooded area used to be surrounded with a tall fence, and the beast made no damage to the citizens.

Baba Yaga misplaced her job. Again she used to be unemployed. However, she had Philemo, her liked cat, and he made her happy....

XII

Extra musings

- The extra high priced you purchase them, the extra precious they shall become.
- A exact quote is an E=mc2 of a poem. A properly poem is an E=mc2 of a story. A true word, at the proper second can blow the world away.
- Poetry cause is to construct connections by using attractive to the senses. When we try to specific our feelings, we open up a connection to appreciation ourselves. When anyone else reads what we express, there's an a chance for a feasible connection.
- A suitable love is like a rash ,That you do not understand the place it got here from. You can cowl it, medicate it But it simply may not go away
- Whether you get knocked down or fall on your own, the journey's no longer over, get again up, hold shifting forward, in no way provide up on what is most important, you may even be amazed by way of the extra advantages you acquire alongside the way.
- Humans are now not created to be owned, freely fallen into every with a signal of devoted love
- Silence speaks extra volumes than complaining ever does.

- Tonight is one of the difficult ones, the place reminiscences of historical conversations and unspoken phrases chunk me up and spit me out like a sobbing fool.
- Love on my own won't therapy the hatred engraved in this planet, however "Action" will. You may additionally have a thousand fantastic intentions in life, if you do now not act on them.
- We by no means areas importantas forgettingourselves.
- Of all the human beings whom I may want to pick from, you are, with no doubt, whom I should by no means undergo to lose.
- It solely hurts this lots due to the fact you cared so much. This plenty ache does no longer stem from a mediocre love, however one that ought to cross the stars. That is a present to be cherished always.
- Life regularly takes greater than it gives. But it can reward you for your struggles and heartbreak with some of the most stunning things. Or now and again it simply hurts and there are training to be learned
- My muse has back but my words nevertheless fail me. I've in no way been in a position to write perfection.
- Don't stroll in the front of me I will now not follow. Don't stroll in the back of me I will now not lead. Just stroll beside me .
- It is no longer a new notion that monsters and demons exist in the human psyche. And thrive there. But how do they get there and why they thrive, that is some thing well worth speakme about.
- Sometimes I prefer to burn the entirety to ashes, simply to rebirth a Phoenix
- Light bends, mild refracts, mild lies to you. Darkness is the remarkable teller of truths.
- Your previous is now not who you are. Your previous solely serve as a tenet to comply with in turning into who you virtually are.
- There is some thing you can usually examine from the previous that can do you suitable nowadays and tomorrow, however do not make the previous your burden.

- The motive why am now not afraid of criticism is due to the fact it is simply a poor terminal; praises make up your advantageous terminal.
- Common feel is a blessing to have in a world of fools
- No one hits rock backside simply due to the fact of their ignorance.They fall into the depths .Because of their arrogance
- There are extra motives to stay than there are humans on this earth. There are many motives for a character to live, solely a lunatic clings to one.
- Always attempt to be the kinder person. In each and every situation, deal with it as a competition. If any one isn't being that excellent to you, preserve in thinking the competition. Be a winner in kindness .Leave.They are not really worth it.
- You've labored too difficult for the little trade you acquired however it is nevertheless constantly short-Lived.
- A existence they desired for too long.Put your self first for once, you in no way wanted any support. The actual energy is in truth.Only readability would convey colorings to shine,otherwise, they only.amalgamate or lay upon one another.

9 798887 836171

Printed by Libri Plureos GmbH in Hamburg, Germany